"

Thousands of tired, nerve-shaken, over-civilized people are beginning to find out that going to the mountains is going home; that wildness is a necessity; and that mountain parks and reservations are useful not only as fountains of timber and irrigating rivers, but as fountains of life.

"

I had nothing to do but look and listen and join
the trees in their hymns and prayers.

When we try to pick out anything by itself, we find it
hitched to everything else in the Universe.

When we contemplate the whole globe as one great dewdrop, striped and dotted with continents and islands, flying through space with other stars all singing and shining together as one, the whole universe appears as an infinite storm of beauty.

Keep close to Nature's heart . . . and break clear
away, once in awhile, and climb a mountain or
spend a week in the woods. Wash your spirit clean.

This grand show is eternal. It is always sunrise somewhere; the dew is never all dried at once; a shower is forever falling; vapor ever rising. Eternal sunrise, eternal sunset, eternal dawn and gloaming, on seas and continents and islands, each in its turn, as the round earth rolls.

The clearest way into the Universe is through a forest wilderness.

Everybody needs beauty as well as bread, places to play in and pray in, where nature may heal and give strength to body and soul alike.

The mountains are calling and I must go, and I will

work on while I can, studying incessantly.

"

As long as I live, I'll hear waterfalls and birds
and winds sing. I'll interpret the rocks, learn the
language of flood, storm, and the avalanche. I'll
acquaint myself with the glaciers and wild gardens,
and get as near the heart of the world as I can.

"

MOUNTAINEERS BOOKS

Enjoy your adventures. And remember to Leave No Trace, www.lnt.org

Printed in Canada

♻ Printed on recycled paper

ISBN 978-1-68051-343-1

www.mountaineersbooks.org

Jeremy Collins roams the earth with sketchbooks in hand, dumping his soul into their pages. Of John Muir, Collins says, "I connect with Muir as a soul who saw the natural world not as a resource for plundering but as hallowed and sacred—not to be worshipped, but revered." Follow Jeremy's adventures on Instagram at @jer.collins and online at jercollins.com

An independent nonprofit publisher since 1960